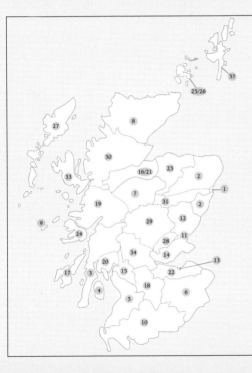

The remaining six books, *Caledonia*, *Distinguished Distilleries*, *Sacred Scotland*, *Scotland's Mountains*, *Scotland's Wildlife* and *The West Highland Way* feature locations in various parts of the country, so are not included in the map list above.

PICTURING SCOTLAND

SACRED SCOTLAND

COLIN NUTT
Author and photographer

2   Sunrise over the Isle of Whithorn symbolises St Ninian bringing the light of Christianity to Alba which, according to tradition, occurred in the 390s. He established the first (known) church here,

SACRED SCOTLAND

resulting in this area becoming known as the cradle of Christianity in Scotland.
See also pages 6, 10 and 11.

Welcome to Scotland's sacred sites!

'Sacred' is not a word that crops up often these days. When it does, it's often in the context of the exasperated exclamation 'Is nothing sacred these days?!' in response to, for example, an act of crass or selfish behaviour that leaves people's sensitivities outraged. The dictionary defines sacred as 'consecrated or held especially acceptable to a deity, dedicated or reserved to some person or purpose; made holy by religious association, hallowed'. So it's interesting that in this allegedly 'post-Christian era' some sense of the sacred stays with us. It certainly helps to explain the continued interest – fascination even – that Scotland's sacred sites elicit from visitors and residents alike.

The theme of sanctity, as expressed in Scotland's ritual and sacred locations, is abundantly evident right across the country and its timeline stretches from earliest human pre-history to present-day practice. The aim of this book is to trace a path through the spiritual journey of Scotland's peoples, from over 5,000 years ago to the here and now. Yes, that's a big challenge for a small tome, but hopefully it will serve to introduce the subject and open the door to deeper investigation.

The journey has to start with recent discoveries at the Ness of Brodgar in Orkney. Within this site of great antiquity (its beginnings going back to at least 3200BC), one of the most impressive

An aerial view of the archaeological excavation of Structure 10 at the Ness of Brodgar, Orkney. 5

discoveries made there is Structure No10, the characteristics of which have led to it being referred to as 'The Temple'. While we can't tell for sure if it was a place of ritual/worship in some nascent form, something of this nature can be inferred from its scale, complexity, the internal layout and features. Structure 10 was built probably around 2900BC but in intermittent use till circa 2400BC.

The link between religion and royalty is another aspect to consider. For centuries, the standing of a monarch was seen as a godly appointment, leading to the concept of the 'divine right of kings'. The traditional meeting place of these ideas was Moot Hill in Perthshire (see p.42), an important religious gathering place for the Picts. It then became the site of an early Christian church, which housed the Stone of Destiny, believed to have been brought to Scotland from Ireland. In due course, it was placed on the Moot Hill and became the coronation place of Scottish sovereigns.

And so from this most ancient beginning, our odyssey around Sacred Scotland follows a broadly chronological trajectory. Following the emerging route of spiritual development and practice requires dotting around virtually the whole country. However, to avoid too many commutes in and out of the big cities, their stories will be covered in a more rounded way.

6 Close up of the Latinus Stone at the 'Whithorn Story', the oldest surviving Christian monument in Scotland. Erected around 450AD, this headstone bears inscriptions about Latinus and his daughter.

In a sense, this book takes us on a form of pilgrimage. What readers will take from it will vary widely. An over-arching sense of pilgrimage down the millennia in search of faith, truth and purpose emerges, from the first Christian evangelists to present-day modelling of their doctrine in today's churches. If the idea of a pilgrimage sounds outdated, bear in mind that pilgrim routes in Scotland are being dusted off and renewed, while some new ones have been established. Annually, around 130,000 people make the long trip to the Isle of Iona, where St Columba established a monastery in 563, and which is now the epicentre of pilgrimage in Scotland. But he wasn't the first of the Christian evangelists from Ireland: that honour goes to Ninian, who arrived in Galloway much earlier – in the 390s, according to tradition. But, for what we are about to explore, may curiosity be aroused, the soul refreshed and faith stimulated.

Detail from the St Ninian window in St Ninian's Priory Parish Church, Whithorn. Ninian kneels in prayer in front of a depiction of the church he built, probably in the late 4th century.

8   This is the main grouping of stones at Calanais, Isle of Lewis, work on which began around 2900BC. Consisting of around 50 stones comprising a circle with central monolith (middle of picture), straight

lines that run approximately north, south, east and west plus the remains of a burial chamber, this amazing site shouts of ritual and reverence for the departed. Other possible uses also postulated.

10 St Ninian's Chapel, Isle of Whithorn. Probably built c.1300, it replaced an earlier, narrower one on this site. It stands within a perimeter wall, as did many early Christian churches.

Above: the nave of the 12th-century Whithorn cathedral, a remnant of the far larger building modelled in **11** the picture below. This shows how the nave (on the left) would have been decorated in medieval times.

12 Columba landed in southern Kintyre, Argyll. Above left: the smooth marks in the stone, known as Columba's footprints; below left: Columba's well; right: Keil Cave, where he may have sheltered.

The 'quiet corner' in Iona Abbey (see front cover), where symbols of Christianity are arrayed: candles, **13** an icon of Mary with the infant Jesus, a cross and an open Bible – aids to prayer and reflection.

14 Left: Iona Abbey Cloister; right: bronze sculpture by Jacob Lipchitz, inscribed 'Jacob Lipchitz, Jew . . . has made this Virgin for the better understanding of human beings so that the Spirit may prevail'.

Top left: the altar of Iona Abbey church decorated for Harvest Festival; below left: symbolic **15** column-top carving, cloister; right: the Abbey church's highly decorated font, on a base of local marble.

16 Left: St Martin's Cross, made between 750 and 800, still stands on its original site in Iona Abbey's grounds; centre: St Columba window in the Abbey church; right: replica of St John's Cross.

St Serf (c.500-580) may have come from the Middle East, but he ended up in Culross (pictured), **17**
Fife. Here he raised the disowned grandson of King Loth, who became St Kentigern, founder of . . .

18 . . . Glasgow. Miraculous works are credited to Kentigern (c.528-614), or Mungo as he became known – see our Glasgow book for more on this. Glasgow Cathedral, built during the 13th to 15th centuries, is

the only medieval cathedral on the Scottish mainland to have survived the 1560 Reformation virtually
complete. St Mungo's Chapel (above) and tomb are located in its extensive and atmospheric undercroft.

20 Just yards from the Cathedral stands the St Mungo Museum of Religious Life and Art. The gallery pictured here features items representing various faiths from around the world and across the times.

Across the Clyde, Govan Old Church has an amazing collection of carved stones from the 9th-11th **21** centuries. The sun stone (right) may be the earliest of them, with both pagan and Christian markings.

22 Continuing the timeline, next comes St Blane (c.530-590). Born on the Isle of Bute, he followed St Catan as abbot of the monastery. The remains of 13th-century St Blane's church stand on the same site.

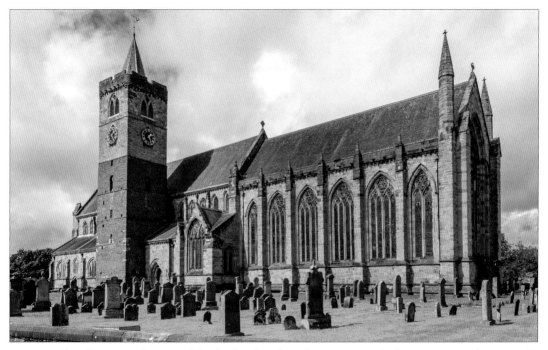

Blane later moved to central Scotland to found another monastery. Its location we now know as **23** Dunblane, where the fine cathedral is home to the memorial for the victims of the infamous event of 1996.

24 St Moluag and his followers established at least 10 churches around Scotland. This one is at Eoropie, on the Isle of Lewis in the Outer Hebrides. The picture on p.1 shows this simple church in its setting.

Famous Eilean Donan Castle takes its name from St Donan (c.550-617), who presumably spent **25** time there. He and 52 monks were massacred at their monastery on the Isle of Eigg.

26 St Machar (c.540-c.600) was one of Columba's companions and is attributed with founding a church on this site c.580. St Machar's Cathedral houses numerous historic artefacts, including this Pictish

cross-stone (left) of c.580, which is probably associated with the original church. St Machar had a reputation for being highly studious, as this stained glass (right) depicts. Fellow monks look on enviously!

28 While in Aberdeen, St Nicholas' Church has its origins in the 12th century. Known locally as the 'Mither Kirk', today's congregation worships in the West Kirk, the section to the left of the spire.

'Holy' wells were often associated with the early saints. Water made safe to drink would have been a **29** blessing indeed in those days. This is St Drostan's Well at Old Aberdour on Aberdeenshire's north coast.

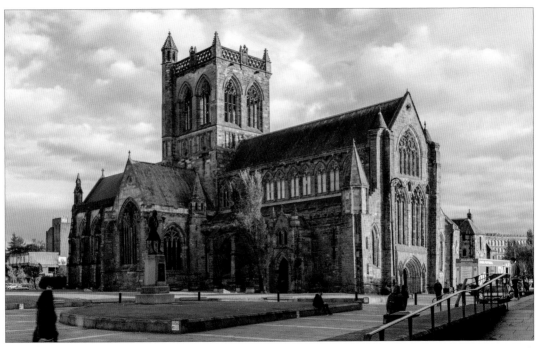

30 Moving back to the Central Belt, Paisley's roots go back to the 6th century when St Mirin (c.565-c.620) established a church, around which a settlement grew up. Its ecclesiastical importance was

consolidated by the founding of the abbey (opposite) in 1163. Pictured above is the Mirin Chapel, with its medieval reredos (the horizontal panel below the window) depicting scenes from his life.

32 In a much more modern style, another part of his Paisley legacy is St Mirin's Roman Catholic Cathedral. Completed in 1931, it was raised to Cathedral status in 1948 with the establishment of Paisley Diocese.

Left: St Molaise (c.566-640) lived as a hermit for some years on this island off Arran, consequently now **33** named Holy Island. Right: an early cross and font associated with him, outside Lamlash Parish Church.

34 St Cuthbert (c.634-687) founded the first church in Edinburgh. The oldest part of today's building is the Memorial Chapel (1775), in which are the Apse (left) and the St Cuthbert window (right).

The main church building dates to 1894 and presents this stunning interior with its highly decorated **35** apse. The stained glass window on the left is by Tiffany of New York. The organ was built in 1899.

36 This picture of the cavernous interior of St Giles Cathedral, Edinburgh, illustrates the contrast between the timeless stillness of the eternity it represents and the un-still bustle of its visitors.

Details from the Thistle Chapel (built 1911) in St Giles: top left: 'misericords' (mercy seats); lower **37** left: an intricately carved cherub; right: cross decorated with the symbols of the four gospel writers.

38 St Maelrubha (642-722) and a group of fellow monks sailed from Ireland to Scotland in 671. After two years of itinerant evangelising, he settled in Applecross and established a monastery at this site.

He continued to travel far and wide around the Highlands and spent time on an island in **39**
Loch Maree (pictured), thereby giving the loch its name – Maree being a conflation of Maelrubha.

40 Many place names relate to the early evangelist-saints, the village of St Fillans on the shores of Loch Earn being another example. St Fillan (c.695-c.770) built a church between here and Dundurn Fort.

The desire to withdraw to remote places for prayer and contemplation is a recurring theme. St Baldred **41**
(c.700-757) had a hermitage on Bass Rock, marked by the later chapel circled in the picture.

42 Scotland's kings were crowned at Moot Hill for centuries (see introduction), starting with Kenneth MacAlpin in 843. The Gothic chapel pictured stands on the site, in the grounds of Scone Palace, Perth.

In 849, relics of St Columba were removed from Iona to protect them from Viking raids and brought **43** to Dunkeld (its Cathedral pictured) by Kenneth MacAlpin, who appointed a bishop there.

44 Left: moving down to Dumfriesshire, the Ruthwell Cross is the most magnificent Anglian cross in Scotland, probably carved in the mid 700s. Right: rather more worn is this statue of St Duthac

(1000-1065), located in a corner of this chapel dedicated to him in the town of Tain, Ross-shire, where 45 he is believed to have been born. After study in Ireland he returned and became a renowned preacher.

46 The Picts have left a legacy of amazing carved stones throughout eastern and northern Scotland. Left: Nigg Stone, housed in Nigg Old Church. Right: a few miles away is Hilton of Cadboll Stone.

Often mysterious, these carvings do however chart the Picts' journey from paganism to Christianity, these **47** designs showing Christian symbols. Left: one of the Aberlemno Stones in Angus. Right: Benvie cross slab.

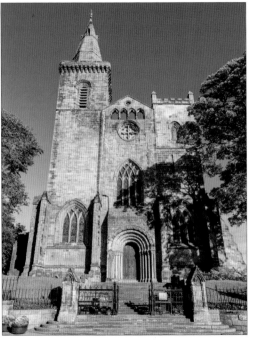

Dunfermline's ecclesiastical beginnings go back to 1070 when, following her marriage to King Malcolm III, Queen Margaret founded a Benedictine community there. Later, their son King David I expanded it into an Abbey, work on which began in 1128. Dunfermline became the burial place of many Scottish Kings and Queens, starting with Margaret in 1093. The most notable royal tomb is that of Robert the Bruce who died in 1329. The Scottish Reformation from 1560 led to much damage being inflicted on the Abbey Church. However, the nave remained in use until 1821, by which time most of the other parts had succumbed to bad weather, decay and subsequent collapse. A new Abbey Church took over from the old in 1821 and now forms the eastern half of the remaining structure.

48 The west end of the medieval part of Dunfermline Abbey Church.

The new (1821) Dunfermline Abbey Church, burial place of Robert the Bruce. The words **49**
'King Robert' are built into the top of the tower as part of the stonework.

Sacrifice is an in-built and unavoidable aspect of Christianity. Sometimes this means believers paying the ultimate price and accepting martyrdom in order to be true to their faith. This is how it turned out for Earl Magnus. In 1117 he and his cousin, Håkon, were the joint Earls of Orkney, but there was considerable enmity between their followers. It was agreed that the two would meet to resolve their differences on the island of Egilsay, each bringing only two ships. Magnus had already gained a reputation for piety and gentleness, having declined to carry arms during a raid on the Welsh some years before. He arrived for the meeting on Egilsay on 16 April 1117 with his two ships, but Håkon brought eight. To cut a grisly story short, to minimise bloodshed between the rival factions, Magnus submitted to execution. When Earl Rognvald came to Orkney twenty years later it was to reclaim his half of the Earldom from Håkon's son, but his lasting legacy was to begin the building of St Magnus Cathedral.

50 The complete but roofless remains of St Magnus Church, located on the spot where he was martyred, on the island of Egilsay. The St Magnus Way, a 55-mile pilgrimage route from Egilsay to Kirkwall

has recently been established. It goes via Birsay, where Magnus was buried, and the ruins of Orphir **51** Church, the unusual circular shape of which is set in the gravel path in the picture above.

52 Remembrance is an integral part of faith; consequently war memorials are often placed next to churches, as here by St Magnus Cathedral in Kirkwall, complete with the 'weeping window' of ceramic poppies.

This is the St Rognvald Chapel at the east end of the cathedral. The three carved figures are Kol, father of the founder (Rognvald), who supervised the earliest work, hence the plumbline; Rognvald, holding a model which helps us visualise the first design; and William, Bishop of Orkney (1102-1168). The communion table is modern, but incorporates six 17th-century panels.

Left: inside St Magnus Cathedral, looking aloft from the Crossing shows how the ascending levels of **53** arcading in the choir, clerestory and triforium reveal the full and majestic height of St Magnus' interior.

54 St Clement's Church, Rodel, Isle of Harris, houses carvings rated as the finest medieval sculpture surviving in the Western Isles. The inset picture shows a carving thought to be of St Clement.

Staying in the Outer Hebrides, Trinity Temple at Carinish on the Isle of North Uist was an important **55** centre of learning in the early medieval period.

56 And on South Uist at Howmore, a peep through the remains of St Dermot's Chapel reveals more examples of round-headed Celtic crosses. Sites like this exude a tranquillity to savour – balm to the soul.

Continuing the island theme, this is Oronsay Priory, on the island of the same name. One of the **57** later Augustinian foundations, its construction goes back to approximately 1325-1350.

58 Left: the kindly protection of trees growing over this headstone is somehow quite moving. Cill Chriosd churchyard, Isle of Skye. Right: only a century old, St Columba's, Isle of Canna, evokes an earlier age.

Back on the mainland: round church towers are a rarity – only two Irish-style examples exist in Scotland, **59** the one in Brechin, Angus (left) and the other in Abernethy, Perthshire (right). Both date from c.1100.

60 The Church of the Holy Rude in Stirling was founded in 1129, although today's edifice was largely built in the 15th and 16th centuries. The coronation of the infant King James VI took place here in 1567.

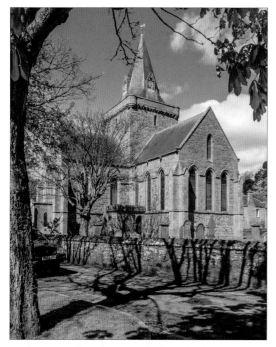

Left: Dornoch's charming little cathedral, begun in 1224, stands at the heart of Sutherland's county **61** town. Right: it contains some of the most beautiful modern glasswork to be found in Scotland.

62 Tarbat in Easter Ross is rich in ancient ecclesiastical history, such that it is known as 'the Iona of the East'. Pictured: a few years ago, a dig was carried out to discover more about Tarbat Monastery.

Early Celts believed Rowan trees had power to protect from evil, so it became common practice to **63** plant them outside churches to ward off evil. These berried Rowans are at Ardchattan Priory, Argyll.

64 Kilmartin Glen, Argyll, is one of the world's most significant archaeological landscapes, which Kilmartin House Museum interprets and exhibits. On the right is a beehive cell like those used by early monks.

In the nearby church and churchyard are displays of carved stones including some well-preserved grave **65** slabs, of which these 14th-15th-century examples give clues about the people for whom they were made.

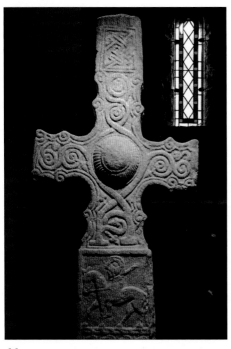

The Dupplin Cross is housed in St Serf's Church in Dunning, Southern Perthshire, itself a remarkable survivor at 800 years old. Described as 'the only complete example of a free-standing cross to survive in Pictish territory', the cross was made for the Pictish King Constantine, who reigned from around 789-820. We know this because a Latin inscription on the back of the cross reads 'Custantin, son of Wuirgust' (Causantin mac Fergusa, or Constantine, son of Fergus). Its survival in such good condition is a minor miracle: until 1999 it stood on a hillside about three miles from Dunning, at Forteviot, the site of a Pictish King's palace. The most arresting feature of the Dupplin Cross is the large domed boss in the centre (there is a similar, more weathered one, on the other side). Historians believe it may represent the sun. It is not a unique feature, as similar forms can be seen on other Pictish stones, e.g. the Aberlemno Stone back on p.47. This one is very slightly tilted, sitting not at right angles to the surface but angled slightly upwards.

A case could be made for starting this book in St Andrews, as legend says St Rule arrived there in 347. A bishop in the Greek city of Patras, he purportedly fled from there with relics (a few bones) of the Apostle St Andrew in 345, fetching up off the coast of Fife two years later. But there are various difficulties with this account; an alternative is that St Acca, formerly Bishop of Hexham, brought St Andrew's relics to Fife sometime after 732. This version (including whether or not the relics really were those of St Andrew) is not a certainty either, not least because it is bound up in ecclesiastical politics about who had the greater claim to be Patron Saint of Scotland – Andrew or Columba. As we know, Andrew won, although he was not made 'official' until 1320. So instead, we look at St Andrews now in order to concentrate on another aspect of the sacred world's influence on medieval life, namely that of education.

The east end of St Andrews Cathedral, viewed from the top of St Rule's Tower, a remnant of St Rule's **67** Church, built c.1120. Work on St Andrews Cathedral began in 1163.

68 And here on the left is St Rule's Tower which, at 33m/108ft, looks down on the east gable of St Andrews Cathedral. The cathedral's west tower can be seen to the right of St Rule's Tower.

St Andrews University owes its existence to a group of eminent ecclesiastics who promoted the idea from **69** 1410. Officially founded in 1413, it's the oldest university in Scotland. Above: St Salvator's College . . .

70 . . . the quad and chapel of which are pictured, was established in 1450. Above is St Mary's College (f. 1538), for which land was given (years earlier) by Bishop Henry Wardlaw (see p.4).

The Scottish Declaration of Independence was signed at Arbroath Abbey in 1320 and St Andrew declared Patron Saint. The original extent of the great abbeys can be appreciated in this model.

72 Above: Kelso Abbey. Scotland's independence led to wars with England for centuries. The birth of Mary, Queen of Scots, in 1542 was seized on by Henry VIII as an opportunity to regain control, as he

saw her as the ideal bride for his son Edward. Treaties to that end were signed in 1543, but England's
Parliament did not ratify them. The Scots' response was to repudiate the treaties, as their mood changed

74 in favour of using Mary to reassert their old alliance with France by offering her as a future bride for the French heir to the throne, Francois. Henry VIII's response to this was to invade Scotland in 1544,

in a campaign that became known as the 'Rough Wooing'. Southern Scotland bore the brunt, with the great Abbeys of Kelso, Melrose (p.73), Jedburgh (p.74) and Dryburgh (above) suffering greatly.

The Reformation. The Protestant Reformation of Christian belief and practice began in 1517 when Martin Luther nailed his *95 Theses* on the door of Wittenburg Cathedral in Germany. The heart of his argument was that scripture alone (the Bible) is the basis for Christian faith and doctrine. He, and other like-minded theologians, took issue with the institutional nature of the Roman Catholic Church in which, as they saw it, too much authority was vested in one man – the Pope – who in turn channelled this power through the hierarchy of the priesthood. This structure distanced the Bible from the people and thus enabled their manipulation by the church.

Protestantism was based on 'The Five Solas', which stated that people's relationship with God should be based on these biblical tenets: by grace alone, through faith alone, in Christ alone, according to Scripture alone and for God's glory alone. This put more responsibility on the faith of the individual which in turn meant anyone should have direct access to the Bible. By Roman Catholicism keeping the Bible in Latin, its interpretation to the masses was in the hands of the priesthood. Protestant reformers led the way in translating the Bible into their languages, to give the people (the literate amongst them anyway) direct access to its teaching.

Human nature being what it is, this revolution in religious practice led to excesses of many kinds. It was never going to be a peaceable process as Roman Catholicism wasn't about to abandon its hegemony without a fight. In Scotland, the first serious outbreak of rebellion took place in St Andrews in 1546. The Roman Catholic Cardinal Beaton had the Protestant reformer George Wishart burned at the stake. In response, a group of Protestants from Fife took the undeniably corrupt Beaton from his home in St Andrews Castle and killed him. Wishart's supporter, John Knox, became the de facto leader of the Scottish Reformation. In 1560, the Scottish Parliament agreed to the Reformed Confession of Faith and legislated the Roman Catholic Church out of legal existence.

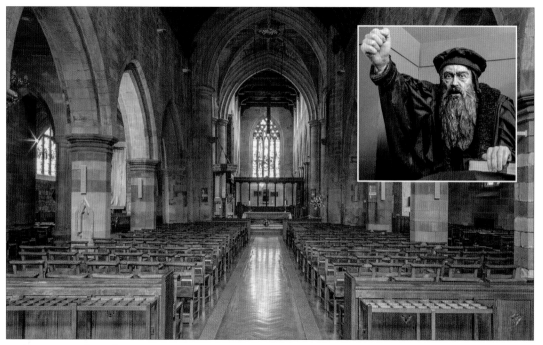

The interior of St John's Church, Perth, where John Knox (inset) preached one of his fiery sermons against idolatry.

78 The destruction of Scotland's Abbeys from 1560 reached even remote locations like Inchcolm Abbey on its island in the Firth of Forth, although here the Chapter House and Warming Room (left) survived.

Sweetheart Abbey in Galloway, named after founder Lady Devorgilla's devotion to the memory of **79** her husband John Balliol, demonstrates more of the Reformation's destructive power.

80 And yet there were extraordinary survivals too. Magdalen Chapel in Edinburgh was one of the last pre-Reformation churches, built 1541–4 for the city's hammermens' (metal workers) guild.

The drive to destroy all forms of religious imagery in churches ('iconoclasm') in the name of stamping out idolatry meant that all stained-glass windows were smashed – except these! The upper two are the Coat of Arms of Mary of Guise (Scottish Queen when the chapel was built) and the Royal Coat of Arms. Below are the arms of founder Michael Maguhen and Maguhen and his wife Janet Rynd.

82 But the most spectacular survivor must be Rosslyn Chapel, a few miles outside Edinburgh. The extraordinary quality, range and volume of the chapel's interior stone carvings are simply astonishing.

Left: the Apprentice Pillar. Right: exterior carvings have inevitably suffered over time, making **83** identification tricky, e.g. the top right may represent the Holy Trinity; lower centre, perhaps a Greenman.

84 Left: Seton Collegiate Church in East Lothian remains roofed and enjoys a tranquil, picturesque setting. Right: the interior houses, in effect, a museum of preserved stone carvings and memorials.

After the Reformation, many churches were remodelled to accommodate the new style of worship. **85** St Mary's in Haddington (where John Knox was born), is the longest parish church in Scotland.

86 Post-Reformation churches were purpose-built. Yester Parish Church in Gifford, East Lothian, was completed in 1710, but kept a link with the previous building of 1492 by retaining its bell.

In Inverness, the Old High Church used to be St Mary's before the Reformation. It was used as a prison **87** after the Battle of Culloden in 1746. Reputedly, some of the prisoners were executed in the churchyard.

88 In 1824, Parliament funded the building of 32 kirks across Scotland. The project was directed by Thomas Telford and they were constructed to a standard design. This example is at Kilchoan in Ardnamurchan.

Duirinish Parish Church (1832) in Dunvegan, Isle of Skye, has been described as a 'jauntier' alternative **89** to the contemporary Parliamentary churches. It is similar in form, but more stylishly finished.

90 The Cathedral of The Isles (1851) on the Isle of Cumbrae, Ayrshire, is the smallest in Britain (the nave seating just 80 people) and an architectural gem. With accommodation available, it's a good place for

a retreat. One of its treasures is this picture, The Adoration of the Lamb. Its allegorical images reference
biblical themes such as the water of life in the fountain and the lamb representing Jesus Christ.

Various denominations (Christian churches with a particular style of worship or emphasis in their teaching) have arisen through the years. The Baptist movement generally dates its beginnings to 1608/9, although its members were not referred to as 'baptists' until 1644. As the name implies, their special emphasis is on the importance of baptism – usually by full immersion – as a means of an individual's demonstration of their commitment to Jesus Christ. The practice goes back to Christ himself, who asked John the Baptist to perform this rite upon him.

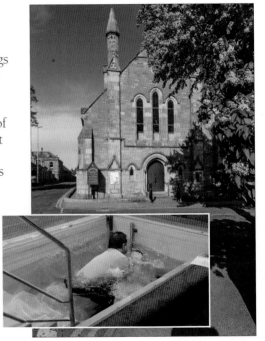

92 Above: the Baptist Church in Elgin, Moray, is one of Scotland's oldest. Below: the minister carries out the practice of baptism by total immersion.

The Thomas Coats Memorial Church in Paisley is Scotland's finest church in the Baptist tradition – **93** indeed, it is known as the Baptist cathedral of Europe. It can be visited by arrangement.

94 The Methodist movement is a group of denominations of Protestant Christianity which derive their inspiration from the life and teachings of John Wesley. This is their Central Hall in Paisley.

The Reformation in Scotland required an alternative church structure. The Church of Scotland was duly established in 1560. It eventually became a 'Presbyterian' church, meaning it was governed by local elders (including the minister) rather than the 'Episcopalian' structure in which a hierarchical system of governance is headed by bishops. This was another way of asserting the difference between the Roman Catholic method and the new Protestant order. But King Charles I, who believed absolutely in the 'divine right of kings', attempted to enforce Episcopalian practice complete with the Book of Canons and the Book of Common Prayer. By February 1638, the Presbyterians in Scotland were facing accusations of treason. They decided that they needed some way of uniting together so they could stand firm against these attacks on their religion. Their position was set out in a document called the National Covenant, support for which led to a war of religion which was, in effect, a precursor to the (English) Civil War.

The National Covenant was first signed at Greyfriars churchyard (left) in Edinburgh on the 28th of **95** February 1638. Within days it had been signed by many of the people of Edinburgh.

96 Edinburgh's Canongate Kirk, established 1688. The stag motif relates to King David I's survival of a hunting accident, which led him to found Holyrood Abbey, which Canongate Kirk eventually replaced.

Left & right: after the Reformation, the manufacture of stained glass died out. It returned to favour **97** in the 19th century. St John's Church in Edinburgh has a sublime collection. Centre: the altar.

98 The 1843 'Disruption' (schism) in the Church of Scotland, over the issue of patronage, began here in St Andrew's & St George's West, Edinburgh: theirs was the first congregation to leave in protest.

The Disruption brought about the formation of the Free Church. The evangelical element had been demanding the purification of the Church and attacked the patronage system, which allowed rich landowners to select the local ministers. Some years of legal action followed and eventually the civil court found in favour of the establishment, i.e. those in favour of continued patronage. So in 1843, 450 evangelical ministers (out of 1,200 in all) broke away, and formed the Free Church of Scotland. Led by Dr Thomas Chalmers (1780–1847), a third of the membership walked out, including nearly all the Gaelic-speakers and the missionaries, and most of the Highlanders. The established Church kept all the properties, buildings and endowments. The seceders created a voluntary fund that enabled the building of 700 new churches and 400 manses (residences for the ministers).

Establishment and new order in Inverness: on the left is the Old High Church (Church of Scotland) and on the right the Free North Church, a member of the Free Church of Scotland.

100 The last stop in Edinburgh is St Mary's Episcopal Cathedral at the city's West End. More precisely, these are its precincts in which stands Old Coates House, part of the cathedral estate.

Moving across to Glasgow, St Andrew's Roman Catholic Cathedral's font of Holy Water reflects the **101** windows above the Altar. A unique feature at the cathedral is the Italian Cloister Garden,

102 a place of remembrance and contemplation. Its mirrored plinths bear inscriptions from the Gospels and Italian poets, set in a grass and slate landscape complete with a 'living water' feature.

Queen's Cross Church in Glasgow's suburbs is the only church designed by Charles Rennie **103** Mackintosh. His inimitable style infuses the whole building, e.g. in the detail on the lectern (inset).

The sacred can appear in the most unlikely places. The Italian Chapel in Orkney was built by Italian prisoners of war during World War Two. They had very little to work with when creating the Chapel, other than two old Nissen huts, unwanted scrap and some concrete. What they created is quite astounding – a unique and wonderful place which is an inspiration to all who visit. Apart from itself, the chapel's other lasting legacy is one of reconciliation. In 1960, Domenico Chiocchetti, creator of the Italian Chapel, returned to Orkney to restore his work. Before he left, he wrote this letter to the people of Orkney: 'Dear Orcadians – My work at the chapel is finished. In these three weeks I have done my best to give again to the little church that freshness which it had sixteen years ago. The chapel is yours – for you to love and preserve. I take with me to Italy the remembrance of your kindness and wonderful hospitality. I shall remember always, and my children shall learn from me to love you.'

104 The façade of the Italian Chapel disguises the utilitarian form of the Nissen hut behind.

The Sanctuary at the Italian Chapel. The paintings in the windows flanking the Madonna and Child **105** mural represent St Catherine of Siena and St Francis of Assisi.

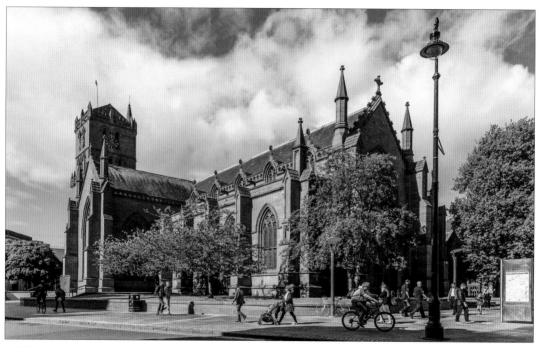

106 These days, churches are having to adapt to changing circumstances and needs. The imposing Steeple Church (now the 'City Churches') in Dundee is not quite what it appears as it does not occupy

the whole building. In contrast to the Gothic architecture, the new multifunctional space enables an **107** active church community to use this space almost every day for different activities and forms of worship.

108 In 2017, the 'Pluscarden 1230 Pilgrimage' recreated the journey made in 1230 by monks from Val des Choux in France to found Pluscarden Abbey near Elgin. Left: Al Monkman and Maria Byron

arrive at Pluscarden carrying the stone from Val des Choux that will be set in the projected new South Range. Opposite right: the arrival procession approaches the abbey. Above: Pluscarden Abbey.

110 In Elgin itself is the unique Biblical Garden, where every plant in the Bible is grown (not necessarily all of them all the time!). Next to it stands Elgin Cathedral, known as the Lantern of the North,

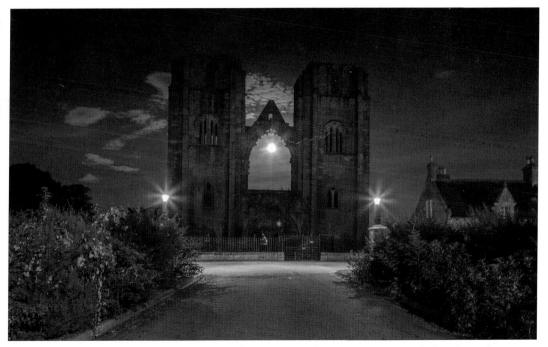

where the combination of nature's lantern and two man-made ones serves to symbolise the Holy Trinity – lights shining in the darkness. A good place to end this exploration of Sacred Scotland.

Published 2019 by Lyrical Scotland, an imprint of Lomond Books Ltd, Broxburn, EH52 5NF
www.lyricalscotland.com www.lomondbooks.com

Originated by Ness Publishing, 47 Academy Street, Elgin, Moray, IV30 1LR

Printed in China

All photographs © Colin & Eithne Nutt except p.5 © Hugo Anderson Whymark and p.83 left © Rosslyn Chapel Trust

Text © Colin Nutt
ISBN 978-1-78818-072-6

Front cover: Iona Abbey; p.1: St Moluag's Church at Eoropie, Isle of Lewis; p.4: statue of Bishop Henry Wardlaw
at St Mary's College, St Andrews; this page: Magnus Macintosh Memorial depicts the four seasons of man
at St Nicholas' Church, Dalkeith; back cover: Inchcolm Abbey

While the Publisher endeavours to ensure the accuracy of information provided, no responsibility
can be taken for errors or omissions. The publisher welcomes information should any be found.